WOVEN WORDS PUBLISHERS *Presents*

THE UNTAMED CACOPHONY

Soumyadeep Bhattacherya was born on 16th May in Icchapur town of North 24 Parganas, where he was brought up in a home of voracious readers. After completing higher secondary education (Kendriya Vidyalaya), he is currently pursuing his bachelor degree (B.Tech) in the field of electronics and telecommunication from KIIT University. Poetry fascinates him ever since. An extreme interest in literature made him into writing. He is also interested in photography and playing various musical instruments.

Contact him on Instagram (@soumyadeepbhattacherya) or on Facebook.

The Untamed Cacophony

SOUMYADEEP BHATTACHERYA

Woven Words Publishers OPC Pvt. Ltd.
Registered Office:
Vill: Raipur, P.O: Raipur Paschimbar,
Dist: Purba Midnapore, Pin: 721401,
West Bengal, India.
www.wovenwordspublishers.net
Email: editor@wovenwordspublishers.net

First published by
Woven Words Publishers OPC Pvt. Ltd., 2017

POETRY

ISBN-13: 978-93-86897-01-5
ISBN-10: 9386897016

Price: $6

Printed and bound in India

ACKNOWLEDGEMENT

I would like to express my gratitude to the many people who saw me through this book; to all those who provided support, Mosiur Rehman sir and woven words publishing. This book is dedicated to my parents and friends, especially to my grandparents and great grandma. Thank you for all your love and support.

Love you all!

Regards,

Soumyadeep Bhattacherya

CONTENTS

1. Candle
2. Drizzling rain and singing beetles
3. Everything was a lie
4. Trip to humanity
5. Forbidden
6. Her dreamy eyes
7. Imperfect
8. Let's kill our dreams
9. Life story
10. Lost humanity
11. Lost love
12. Missing
13. Mask
14. Palestine
15. Portrayal
16. Rules of the world
17. Secret diary
18. Stop
19. Sweet friends
20. Broken
21. Puzzle
22. The sparrow
23. Wait till I learn to lie
24. Window
25. Secured

1 Candle

Face just started to breeze in,

In turn of the candle's tear;

Adornment of the ring flashed,

Into my eyes like a thunder spark;

Wax melts to foster her sprout,

 The half shaded face reveals,

To be a divine lady;

Fine tune of anklet mimics,

The song of red chrysanthemums;

An urge from Elysium made,

2. Drizzling rain and singing beetles

Drizzling rain and singing beetles

The smoky glass panes of beating breaths

The dimmed rosy flickering shiny flakes

Hair covering half on her ambitious eye

The dripping chromes from the perfect strokes

As of the lashes holds reflecting beads of pain

Sailing in the ocean of tempest whirls

When gossamery piece blown by mystical
breeze

 Amaryllis bloom to endorse the beauty

Moon yearn to finesse the stage

Time stopped to treasure the moment

Portrait of evil love enshrined forever in his
poetry.

3. Everything was a lie

It was just a mere lie,

The time we shared that ordinary night,

Under the flaming star's flare

Remember, I used to portray you

As the palate of rising colors

Eyes were hiding behind the monochrome layer

Moments beneath the chandelier

Floating and colliding midair;

Touched and scattered like ashes of an ivory

Rubbed, scrubbed and days passed

Memories faded with each passing day

Still, the essence mists that expectation pay.

The sun of soul shines even brighter.

4. Trip to humanity

The pale yellow little girl glistened

Soaked in water full of intentional poison

To gift the wondrous woman, a present

In an idiotic man made glass vase

Apparently, you may think that

She is much more blessed than you.

But!! You can't feel the pain,

When this cruel world eludes to separate

From her mother, at such a tender age

Each strand was shaved to give a look

A look of pain, hidden to look beautiful

The same being who hurt the flower

When got hurt in love,

Rends petals to show the wrath

He and she somehow managed to sort

Only mother couldn't express her thoughts

A five-day tour to humanity finally ended

Hope of her return silently faded.

5. Forbidden

God made me but you didn't accept me

From each sector why we are abolished

Thrashing away like a wrecked piece

I am forced to do this

As nobody accepted me as it is

Selling my body I earn a living

Quotes are buried down with no meanings

I wonder, why people say such things

When it looks alluring only in pricey coverings

I have no objection but,

Do not inject any false impression

As I have lost all hopes

Pleading that future not follows

Ultimately, heart's beating with inner sorrows.

6. Her dreamy eyes

Her dreamy eyes are numb

That reflects the mystery hidden

A thousand dazzling galaxies that,

Takes leap into sweetest fairytale

Smile can snatch the sunshine,

To make flower dance in rain

The feel of feathery hair,

Slips from mind now and then

Eyes could narrate untold stories

Of hundred unfinished chapters of a tale

7. Imperfect

I can't claim that you

 To be the prettiest

Neither have the ye perfected one.

 But I love the wilderness in you

From each stroke of the kohl

To the matte finish of your lips

I love the imperfect one.

The tie hold hostile, adds spark to the

Rejuvenating wondrous imperfect beauty

Thou the imperfect is the perfect beauty

That's what I want to see.

8. Let us kill our dream

We are born to satisfy others dream

As because ours are not professional

And that also too main stream

Money, car and home are my laden needs

No one cares what I really love

It's only the stereotype that matters

My bad, I can't get into a government college

Actually, I nurtured brain into a hybrid one

At least I made into a money raptor

I used to sit on the first bench

But slowly shifted to last

As playing with wires is not a cup of tea

Semester passed like old reel of film

Sat on a static car and background changed

Gear shifted and rooms changed

Acceleration paddle of mine is still broken

Scribbling theorem never got into my head

The theater goes and I enjoyed, not really!!

Hundred pieces of files I donated to get markings

Like a local train schedule of life goes on

Poems are hidden between the folds of boring verse.

9. Life story

Hi, I am a girl

Probably of your age

Or may not be

I have seen this world much closely

Coped up with tricks too

That's why I am standing before you

Aah! I forgot to tell my name

Because, there is no need

As my hand speaks

Its cuts and bruises tells a different story

That can steer you beyond the limits

Of your dammed imaginations

Breaking the taboos of the society

Many of them teased and spoke behind my back

But I didn't paid any heeds

When I reached the peak

Everyone applauded and

Praised my deeds

10. Lost humanity

A charming city with joy around

Everyone was busy in their own schedule

There was a different kind of flavor

At miles away from this lively hub

A decision was taken, nobody ever thought

This sky blazing would turn tarnish in an hour

People will choke in their poisonous air

Sitting on the seat with the launch pad in hand

I decided to portray this greedy world

In no time everything trashed

With the cracking sound and a fire flash

I am medaled for this difficult job

When I stand before the mirror, loud voices of

The unborn fetuses point me as a traitor.

11. Lost love

Since then nothing really changed

The backyard garden and broken panes

Maybe we are now a little bit shy

After ten long years, I am at destination

The place with lush green stretches

Sun drenched roads with guided canopy

All I missed these long years are now at par

I can hear the welcome song and sense it

The moment of innervations was too near

As we promised to meet right here

It's somewhat awkward as now I have long beard

Still the hope that she could recognize, I feared.

A small boy called my out name and hugged from behind

Hand was tightly gripped by the awaited star of today's night

As I left the rose in the middle of quite road,

As her smile can quench all my sorrows

12. Missing

Billions of stars are just hanging above head

The small girl tries to solve the tricky puzzle

Looking up, dozing on her cushioned bed.

She wonders how a bird can fly with its wings,

But she cannot fly with her hands and limbs.

To listen from the speaking tree about changing scenes,

In her soft bursting and innocent bubbled dreams.

Now, she is a teen

These questions are just scrap,

Not meant for technology geek, sweet sixteen.

 Somehow we all grew up, over the missing link.

13 Mask

One day I will tear off the mask

The one painted with innocence

Putting forth the nudity of reality

Every time you stand in front of me

A shadow searches for serenity

You are the dark cursed beauty

Cursed by hundreds of unborn fetuses

Leaving the mother's lap barren

I feel the negative forces in me

To reflect the reflection of you

Inside my half ridden rib bone

I won't plead guilty or have had grief

If my hands choke you to death

If it prevents any loss to humanity

I am the mirror,

This is not meant to show

Your pretty, lusty looks anymore

It's time for the revolutionize

To break the fourth wall of illusion,

And invade the land of truth.

14. Palestine

Palestine's easels are no more like before

Lake side swans still visits, but not us anymore

Maybe generation drift was too steep for a roll.

The rush for your first sight, was heart wrenching

The dandelion blown relates the bridge interpolating.

I am writing, backing my head on the hundredth floor's wall

The one behind the garden of dreams, witnessed partitioning

 Hugs and kisses are just excuses to sway into the harmony

The beat of your heart popping into my mind now and then;

Mingled into the day dreams breaking the solitaire

Taper shed its tear for every memory clasped

Still the hand softened to cast the die

It's better not to desist for the seventh heaven.

15. Portrayal

I don't know her.
When I stir,
my mind recapture
tardily becomes blurring.

The touch of feathers in forehead,
Shadow in her eye,
Yen to fly,
makes me high.

Glide in the free air,
and sail her fathomable hair,
was just a fairytale,
now, no more real.

A call for aid,
continuously reverberates,
slowly fades,
A dream culminates.

16. Rules of the world

After the little feet kisses the earth

Since, you stood by us all along

When the sky rages high

I made you feel the drizzle

Facing my breast to the storm

You enjoyed the rays during crystal cold

I spread my arms to resist the scorching soul

Love in the air, when you dress up in crimson

I want to see you evergreen ever and forever

Expectation is a mere realization

In factual distinction, of the concocted world

Ultimately, memories cherish

Until the flames from the dark barks calm.

17. Secret diary

I was five,

I always wondered why he used to beat,

It's always the silence that speaks.

Her body became a mere stone,

Seems she can't take any more.

Then I am nine,

Stood in a line with makeup, fine!

They checked me,

And bided for a handful penny

There was an excitement to be free

Took time to realize, stuck in the same tree!

I am eighteen!

Now can relate

The same story will repeat,

Till my death

There is no point to escape,

Even the society will treat as a dumped cake.

So, the journey is up to here,

Asserts the soul of a dead scripter

18. Stop

Everything is stand and still

No leaves, nothing is moving

The chirping birds paused in air

Playing with the winds that care;

The ball is about to kiss the ground

Smile on faces put the extra charm.

Racing motors freezes mid road.

 Gosh, the cat again managed to fetch

A fish from the waterlogged street

Workers stopped building highs

That would steal the rays thereby.

I am walking alone in the world

World full of dismay and maze

Free, yet not free to get lost.

Wish I could play the blossom in loop,

To enjoy the calm, yet delightful fruit

Every time when I feel down and

Quitting nest inside mind's room

19. Sweet friends

Unbitted sweet friends are the magic,

The shadow was unexplored beneath lids.

Presence of innocent nude curves makes me

Feel the minion volts of current passing through spines.

Thought executing; difficult to hide inside my heart;

Oh, I forgot about your well-crafted busts.

Twigs slips flawlessly through your conditioned,

Yet messy kinda hair that hypnotized, led me to an illusion.

Sun sets but not the adorners, as the city lights sparks

Give the perfect blend with your glowing moon face and

The traces of stars were casted on the flexuous Tames.

A beat skip, when I sense your pursy finger's heat,

I wish I could make gear shift, riding like a trained equestrian.

When the body gets reeked up under the dim light,

The ice slowly melts inside the glass of chilled wine.

Dawn wishes; it shouldn't be a falls purpose dream last night.

Bruises were felt all over my inked neck,

Betcha! A damn fair game was played.

20. Broken

The broken bond, the lost fond

The broken clock that blocks

Path of promised togetherness

The locks from lips to hand,

Now widens the distant eyes

Leaving roses of life in pain

It's not gap that push apart

Maybe the scented flavor does?

Changed the perseverance

In a parallel way of leading life

 Trying hard to make things easy,

In most distressful broken phase of life

21. Puzzle

The puzzle pieces are now lost

Lost in the darkness of past

Some which fits perfectly before

Finds difficult to fit in now

We claim situation to be the responsible

But it's us who forgot to make space in.

Till now ease of access made us dependent

Making lame and dismantle

Finally abandoned midway, behind the hues

Some left it shattered and misplaced,

Many couldn't make it.

The one who continued trying;

Though, if not able to reach the top,

Still way ahead on the way,

Where others got puzzled, lost hope

At the Xing; the street flowed into current.

22. The sparrow

The little sparrow went out a day

Searching for food in a hazy way

For the first time she looked down the earth

And amazed to see that trees disappeared

There was a scorching heat

As day by day, ocean of concrete increased

She understood an important thing

In this world full of dismay

Humans can do anything

Killing brotherhood, they earn a living

How can we expect from this living being?

One thing she made it clear

The end of this world is near

The sparrow went to search for hay

Never thought that culinary will betray

23. Wait till I learn to lie

Wait till the framed scene change till

The last nail nailed into the coffin of truth

An opaque film of lie will cover us bit by bit

The sun won't glow bright; moon won't give beliefs

The raindrops will push it through the land

Souls will be trapped under the treacherous sand

Gold and gem couldn't save from their raging hands

When the existence of goodwill sell out

It's only a brave heart lie, which will shout.

24. Window

The cuckoo sings the sweet song of love

Somehow mixed into the harsh dismayed face

Sweet smile she carries is not of happiness

But the storm she faced at midway alone

The red roses of bed turned slowly tarnished

Moon hid behind the cloud and betrayed

She be the lone walker on the way of
melancholies

Trying to pave paths with stick of hope and
support

Wounds healed as the dark tunnel finally came
to an end

And now when she pulls out the window of
mirror

I can see the rejuvenating life very clear

25. Secured

I remember the day

We felt secured in your arms

Curdling and playing with your hairs

I remembered the day

When the blazing sun plays hide-and-seek

The beautiful lady with crown spreads love

With her gracious voice

There was an unfathomable beauty

No words to describe. The beauty... The love.

Today I don't want to remember

When she stands still and soulless

The beautiful lady is now lost

Lost in the mist of modernization

No one saw her tears, left behind scars

We are so advanced, still lifeless

So much chaos, but still calmness

Wrapped around us,

Don't think too much

Move on,

Money and power rule the world.

Forgetting

Love adheres it All... Adheres it All.